THE ODDS ARE IN YOUR FAVOR

when you let world-renowned authority Terence Reese clue you in on the winning strategies for all the popular, exciting, and potentially profitable games of chance you will find in casinos from Atlantic City to Monte Carlo.

Is it better to bank your money on the deal of the cards, the throw of the dice, or the spin of the wheel? Should you make a few big bets or a lot of little ones? Which casinos offer better odds, American or European ones? Here, from a master, is everything you need to know about playing and—

WINNING AT CASINO GAMBLING

Correct odds • House percentages • Playing strategy
Official up-to-date rules • Timing your bets •
And much, much more

Terence Reese is the leading card player in Great Britain and, according to *The New York Times*, "the world's best bridge player." He's played for Great Britain in all the world championship matches, and is generally considered an expert in every kind of card game and gambling game as well as in backgammon. He has written more than fifty books and his work has been translated into all the European languages.

D0424362

WINNING CASINO GAMBLING

an international guide

by
TERENCE REESE

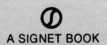

A SIGNET BOOK

SIGNET
Published by the Penguin Group
Penguin Books USA Inc., 375 Hudson Street,
New York, New York 10014, U.S.A.
Penguin Books Ltd, 27 Wrights Lane,
London W8 5TZ, England
Penguin Books Australia Ltd, Ringwood,
Victoria, Australia
Penguin Books Canada Ltd, 10 Alcorn Avenue,
Toronto, Ontario, Canada M4V 3B2
Penguin Books (N.Z.) Ltd, 182–190 Wairau Road,
Auckland 10, New Zealand

Penguin Books Ltd, Registered Offices:
Harmondsworth, Middlesex, England

Published by Signet, an imprint of New American Library,
a division of Penguin Books USA Inc.

This is an authorized reprint of a hardcover edition published by
Sterling Publishing Co., Inc.

First Signet Printing, April, 1979
20 19 18 17 16 15 14 13

 REGISTERED TRADEMARK—MARCA REGISTRADA

Printed in the United States of America

Contents

Foreword

Anybody entering a casino for the first time will find a variety of games in progress that at first sight seem puzzling. Most of them are basically simple, but all contain a host of conventions and special procedures. The first task of this book is to explain the most popular games in a way that will enable a newcomer to play any of them correctly and intelligently.

The second task is to explain the *best* way to play these games. The odds offered to the customer vary considerably. At Craps, for example, some types of wager are twenty times as unprofitable as others. It is well to know!

One virtue that may be claimed for the book is that it is wholly factual and impartial. The title, *Winning at Casino Gambling*, is fair in the sense that the player is informed exactly where his best chances lie, and how good they are. In particular, a just place is accorded to those who peddle staking systems and seem capable of making fortunes for everyone except themselves.

In the analysis of American and European gambling, and in all that concerns odds and statistics, the author has had invaluable assistance from E. Lenox Figgis, of England and the Isle of Man, a noted expert in this field.

TERENCE REESE

Blackjack

'81 LAYOUT

DEALER

BLACK JACK PAYS 3 TO 2

DEALER MUST DRAW TO 16 AND STAND ON ALL 17'S

INSURANCE PAYS 2 TO 1

BLACKJACK

(Also called *Twenty-One*)

1. Nature of the Game

Name of the game

The game originated in France, where it is called *vingt-et-un* (twenty-one). Blackjack is a specific holding (two cards totalling 21), but this is now the common term for the game in all casinos.

Object of the game

The dealer (an employee of the casino) gives cards in turn to his opponent (the player) and himself. Both sides attempt to get as close to a card count of 21 as possible without exceeding it.

Layout of the table

The players sit in a semi-circle facing the dealer. (See page 9.)

The seven rectangular boxes are the places where the seven players (if the table is full) place their wagers. Currency or chips placed between the boxes are not part of the game but requests for change, either currency into chips or chips into chips of a different denomination.

Placing wagers

To make a bet, a player places chips or currency in the wager box in front of him. A notice beside or above the table will indicate minimum and maximum stakes, as for example, minimum $1, maximum $100. (In Nevada, $500 is generally the maximum.) When all seats are not occupied, a player may place additional wagers in other, empty, boxes, thus in effect playing two or more games.

Value of the cards

The four suits have no significance in the game. Cards 2 to 9 have their face or "pip" value. Tens, Jacks, Queens and Kings all count 10. For brevity, they are described as 10-value cards. An Ace counts either 1 or 11, at the player's option. Thus a player who holds an Ace and a 7 may treat his hand as 18 or (for the moment) as 8. (We will see later that the dealer does not have the same options.)

The two stages of play

To understand the nature of the game, let us see what happens if any two persons decide to play a hand of Blackjack against one another. One of them (the dealer) gives a card to his opponent (the player), a card to himself, which is turned face up, and a second card to the player and to himself. The cards given to the player may be open or concealed—it makes no difference to the subsequent play. This is the first stage.

Now the player, who has seen the dealer's card, decides whether to "stand" on or "stick" with the cards he holds or to ask for another one, called "hitting" or asking to "be hit."

Face-up Dealing from the Shoe

In this example the dealer shows a King, which counts 10. The player who has K K, worth 20, decides to stand, since the only way in which he could improve his hand would be to draw an Ace, counting 1. The player with 8 4 decides to be hit. If he draws another low card he is entitled to ask for a fourth, and even fifth or sixth, card. However, IF THE PLAYER GOES OVER 21, he is said to "break" or "bust" and loses his money. If the player stops short of 21, or has 21 exactly, the dealer then turns up his own second card. The dealer may in certain circumstances continue to draw. If the dealer goes over 21, he loses. If not, the totals are compared, the higher total winning. If the totals are equal, the hand is a tie or "stand-off" or "push," neither side winning.

There are various SPECIAL SITUATIONS, which will be described in due course.

The dealer's advantage

The dealer's basic advantage lies in the fact that the player is the first to be submitted to the hazard of going bust. (Of course, a player can avoid breaking by declining to be hit when a high card would put his total over 21, but this would often not be the best playing strategy.) This, considered by itself, is a substantial advantage, but it is balanced by (a) certain restrictions on the dealer's play and (b) certain bonuses or options available to the player, allowing him to profit from promising situations.

The skill factor

Blackjack is different from other casino games in that it contains a skill factor. First, there is a basic playing strategy that can be applied to any situation that may arise in the game. Second, there is scope for expertise, resulting from observation of all cards previously seen. To give a brief example of what is meant, suppose that the dealer is using two decks and that, after half the cards have been played, it can be calculated that the remainder of the deck contains an unusually high, or unusually low, proportion of 10-value cards. Such calculation has an effect on the best playing strategy.

2. Casino Procedure

Number of decks used

In the early days Blackjack was played with a single deck of 52 cards, dealt by hand. Use of a single deck offers distinct possibilities to a player who is capable of remembering the cards and altering his strategy according to the content of the few cards left towards the end of the deal. To minimize this advantage, some casinos nowadays use four decks, shuffled together. Although this favors the house, it is only by a few hundredths of a per cent. However, it makes precise calculation more difficult for the player and less effective. Moreover, the dealer is not obliged to use the entire deck: he may use only about two-thirds, or even less.

At almost all casinos the dealer will use a device known as a "shoe," from which the dealer slides out the cards one by one.

The shuffle, cut and deal

The cards are shuffled in full view of the players. The dealer invites any one of the players to cut by placing a joker or plastic blank somewhere towards the back of the deck.

How Player Cuts Multiple Deck for Dealer

The deal begins when all players have made their wagers. The top card is taken from the shoe, exposed (or in most casinos not exposed) and then "burned." That is to say, it is placed on one side in the discard tray.

Face-Down Dealing from the 4-Deck Shoe

The dealer gives the first card (after the burnt card) to the player sitting at First Base on the right of the semi-circle (dealer's left side), and continues in clockwise order, one card to each player, then one to himself, face up. He deals a second card to each player and a second card to himself, face down. If the dealer's up card is a 10-value or an Ace he looks at his second card, for the reason explained in the next section.

Depending on the practice of the casino, the cards to the players may be given face down or face up. When they are face down, the player picks them up with one hand to peek at them. When they are face up, he does not touch them. Tactically, it makes no difference whether the cards are dealt face down or face up, because the dealer's play is controlled by fixed rules.

When dealer or player has Blackjack

When either the dealer or a player holds 21 in two cards, by way of an Ace and a 10-value, he is said to hold "Blackjack." This leads to special situations.

First, if the dealer's first card is a 10-value or an Ace he may immediately look at his hidden or "hole" card. If this card gives him Blackjack he turns them over and play ceases. Any player who also holds Blackjack ties, and the rest lose their stake. In some casinos the dealer does not peek at his hole card or expose his Blackjack until later.

Second, a player who holds Blackjack displays it when his turn comes and (unless the dealer also holds Blackjack) is paid at odds of 3 to 2. If he has wagered $10, for example, he wins $15 for a total of $25.

The option to take insurance

You may have noted, in the diagram showing the layout of the table, the words "insurance pays 2 to 1." The opportunity to insure occurs when the dealer's first card is an Ace. Before dealing any more cards, after all the players and the dealer have received two cards, the dealer will ask "Insurance?" A player may now hedge by taking insurance against the dealer giving himself Blackjack by turning up a 10-value to go with the Ace. The player insures that he will not lose in this event, by putting up a stake half the value of the original stake.

If the dealer, after insurance has been taken, has Blackjack he pays out 2 to 1 on the insurance bet, which means in effect that the player gets all his money back. If the dealer does not complete Blackjack, the insurance bet is lost.

The wisdom or otherwise of taking insurance is discussed in a later section.

When a player wishes to stand

When all the players have been dealt two cards, the dealer will glance at the player on the right of the semi-circle (First Base). This player will signify whether he wishes to stand or be hit. A player whose cards total 17 or more (counting an Ace as 1) will invariably stand, and he may stand on less. This will depend on his present total and on the card shown by the dealer.

When the cards have been dealt face down, a player wishing to stand will slide his cards under his stake. When cards have been dealt face up, a player who wishes to stand should make a negative gesture and not utter a word such as "stand" or "no." (Dealers are supposed to respond to hand gestures only, but in some casinos at small bet tables this rule is not followed.)

When a player wishes to be hit

A player who wishes to take an extra card in the hope of improving his hand will signify this by word or gesture. The act of scratching one or more fingers towards himself conveys this meaning. Also if cards are face down, waving the cards with your hand (not just your fingers) achieves the same thing. A player may continue in his turn only to ask for cards and these will be given to him until he "stands."

When a player breaks

When a player's total has gone past 21 he has lost. If his cards were face down he turns them up and the dealer places them in the discard tray, taking the wager at the same time. If the cards are face up, the dealer will simply pick them up and place them in the discard tray.

Hard hands and soft hands

As mentioned earlier, Aces may be counted as 1 or 11. A hand containing no Ace, or a hand where an Ace is counted as 1, is called a hard hand. Whenever an Ace may be counted as 11, the hand is a soft hand. Examples:

K 10 is a "hard" 20.

A 9 is a "soft" 20 because the Ace is being counted as 11.

The distinction is important because a player with, say, 2 5 A may either count his hand as a "soft 18" and take no more cards or may count it for the moment as 8 and continue to be hit. (When assessing your hand, provisionally, count Ace as 11 if you can without going over 21.)

Dealer's hitting rule

When all the players' hands have been completed, the dealer turns up his "hole" card and plays out his hand according to fixed rules. The dealer must "buy" or draw to 16 or less. The dealer must stand on any hard 17, but in some casinos must draw to soft 17. (In most casinos the dealer must stand on both hard and soft 17. In this case, a dealer whose first three cards are, say, 4 2 A, giving him a soft 17, does not have the option, as would a player, to continue to take cards.)

Settlement

If the dealer breaks, going over 21, all players still in the game, not having broken themselves, are paid out at even money. A player who has staked $5 wins $5. When the totals are equal, the hand is a tie. The dealer will leave the player's stake in the wager box for the next hand, but the player may withdraw or alter it if he wishes.

3. Player's Basic Strategy

We have described the general procedure of the game and turn now to the best way to play it.

The decision whether to hit or stand is often close, but "best is best" and all these decisions have been determined by computer testing. These rules for the player are invariable:

(a) When the player's count is 11 or less he will always ask to be hit. This is obvious because he cannot go bust on his next draw and may improve. Remember that if he draws an Ace he can count it as 1, not 11.

(b) When the player's count is hard 17 or more he always stands. It is true that if the dealer is showing, say, an 8 there is a strong possibility that he will draw a 10-value card and end up with 18, so the player may be tempted to draw, hoping for a low card, preferably a 4. On balance, however, it is better to stand on 17 and hope that the dealer will go bust.

When the player holds a hard 12 to 16

The difficult—or rather, unwelcome—decisions occur when the player holds a hard 12 to 16, known as a "stiff." A hard hand, remember, is one that does not contain an Ace that can be counted as 11. Now the first card shown by the dealer is highly relevant. The dealer may hold one of two types, "high" or "low." Cards from 7 to Ace are high, from 2 to 6 are low.

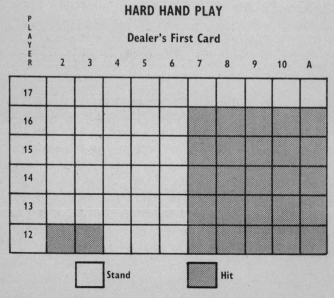

HARD HAND PLAY

PLAYER

Dealer's First Card

	2	3	4	5	6	7	8	9	10	A
17										
16						Hit	Hit	Hit	Hit	Hit
15						Hit	Hit	Hit	Hit	Hit
14						Hit	Hit	Hit	Hit	Hit
13						Hit	Hit	Hit	Hit	Hit
12	Hit	Hit				Hit	Hit	Hit	Hit	Hit

□ Stand   ▓ Hit

When the dealer's card is high, it is right for you to draw when you hold 12 to 16. Of course, it is annoying to draw to a stiff and go bust, then see the dealer go bust in turn. Many players habitually stand on 16, but this is fractionally wrong. Reflect, always, that the most *likely* draw by the dealer is a 10-value because there are four of these in every 13. This is why it is right in principle to draw to 16, even though it is 8 to 5 on that you will go bust.

The situation is quite different when dealer's card is low, from 2 to 6. Now your best chance, with two small exceptions, is to stand on 12 to 16. Again it is tempting, with 12, to draw, as any card from 5 to 9 will give you a pat hand, while 2 3 and 4 will leave you no worse off (you will have to hope that dealer will go bust). Nevertheless, with 12, it is right to stand when dealer shows a 4 5 or 6 (his worst cards). If dealer turns up a 2 or 3 it is right for you to draw to 12. A dealer showing a 2 or 3 is less likely to move into the dreaded area (for him) of 15 or 16, so these are fair cards for the dealer.

It is important to understand the reasons for various plays because they are then much easier to remember.

The diagram opposite shows the correct play for all hard hands. This is the most important diagram in the chapter, because these situations occur all the time.

To sum up once again: **When dealer's card is high (7 to Ace) you draw on 12 to 16.**

When dealer's card is low (2 to 6) you stand on 12 to 16, except that you draw to 12 when dealer's card is 2 or 3.

When the player holds a soft hand

The principles of play are quite different when the player holds a soft hand, containing one or more Aces which can be counted as either 1 or 11.

Suppose that dealer shows what for him is a poor card, a 4 5 or 6, and your first three cards are 4 2 A. You can count your hand as 17 and might be tempted to stand, as you can at least tie with 17. However, in the long run, 17 or 18 is a losing hand for a player. You would do better to draw, as though your total were 7. If you draw a 5 6 7 8 or 9 you will be in the zone of 12 to 16 and will have to stand, but you will be worse off only to the extent that you will now lose to dealer's 17 instead of tying. It is correct to draw to the soft 17, with chances to make a better total.

You should normally stand on a soft 18, but there are two exceptions. When the dealer shows a 9 or 10-value there is a danger that he will make 19 or 20, and it now becomes correct to draw to a soft 18.

This diagram indicates the best play with a soft hand:

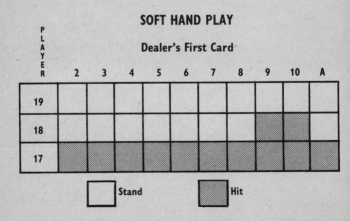

SOFT HAND PLAY

PLAYER	Dealer's First Card									
	2	3	4	5	6	7	8	9	10	A
19										
18								Hit	Hit	
17	Hit	Hit	Hit	Hit	Hit	Hit	Hit	Hit	Hit	Hit

☐ Stand   ▨ Hit

To sum up: **Always draw to a soft 17. Stand on 18 except when dealer shows a 9 or 10-value. Stand on 19.**

The effect of position at the table

Where you sit at the table makes no difference to your basic strategy. Also, the actions of other players do not alter your chances. Players will often grumble when the player who is last to speak before the dealer does not follow standard procedure, but whether his unorthodox play will be beneficial or otherwise for the rest of the table is purely a matter of chance. This is easy to see if you think of it in this way: whether the dealer gives himself the 83rd or 84th card of the deck does not change the odds.

4. Special Situations (Proposition Bets)

The player has two additional options that are slightly to his advantage. Having seen his own first two cards and the dealer's first card, he may in certain circumstances increase his original bet. These are known as Proposition Bets. The exact rules vary from one casino to another but are always displayed.

Doubling down with a hard hand

In some casinos a player has the option of doubling his bet upon receiving his first two cards. It is wise to accept this option when your first two cards total 11 10 or 9. You then place additional chips in your wager box and, having done this, are allowed to draw only one card.

The best initial count for the player is 11, because he cannot go bust and has a good chance to draw a 10 and make 21. With 11 it is always correct to double, even when the dealer has turned up an Ace. You have the advantage because you know that dealer has *not* made Blackjack. (Remember that when dealer's first card is an Ace or 10-value he looks at his hole card to see if he has Blackjack.)

With 10 you should double against any card from 2 to 9, but not against 10 or Ace. With 9 you may double when the dealer holds a relatively poor card, from 2 to 6. You may think that you have the advantage against dealer's 7 or 8, but this is not so because you are allowed to be hit only once. It would be particularly annoying to draw 2, making 11, and be obliged to stand.

This diagram illustrates the best play with a hard hand:

HARD HAND PLAY

P L A Y E R

Dealer's First Card

PLAYER	2	3	4	5	6	7	8	9	10	A
11	▓	▓	▓	▓	▓	▓	▓	▓	▓	▓
10	▓	▓	▓	▓	▓	▓	▓	▓		
9	▓	▓	▓	▓	▓					

▓ Double Down   ☐ Do not Double Down

Summing up, **you always double with 11; with 10 except against 10 or Ace; with 9 against any low card (2 to 6).**

Doubling down with a soft hand

A player who has been dealt A 8 or A 9 should always play his hand as a pat 19 or 20. It would be a mistake to double down because the player would then be obliged to draw a card and might end up with a poor total.

With other soft combinations, from A 2 to A 7, it is correct to double when the dealer shows 4 5 or 6 and is quite likely to break. A double is also recommended on A 7 against dealer's 2 and on A 6 or A 7 against dealer's 3.

This diagram illustrates doubling down strategy with a soft hand:

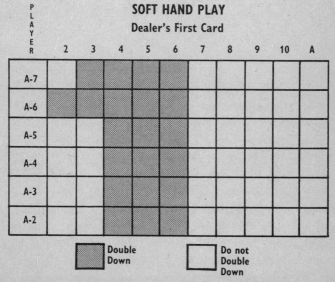

SOFT HAND PLAY
Dealer's First Card

Player rows: A-7, A-6, A-5, A-4, A-3, A-2; Dealer's First Card columns: 2 3 4 5 6 7 8 9 10 A

Legend: Double Down / Do not Double Down

To repeat, **with A 2 to A 7 you double down against dealer's bad cards, 4 5 and 6. Double is also favored with A 6 against 2 and 3, with A 7 against 3.**

Splitting pairs

When a player is dealt two cards of equal value, a pair, he may split them and play two hands separately. He puts up an additional stake (the same amount as the original bet), as shown in this illustration:

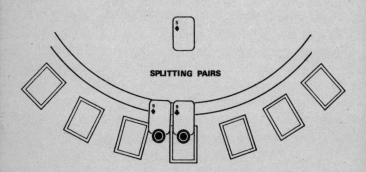

SPLITTING PAIRS

These are the usual rules concerning pair splitting:

(a) It is much to the player's advantage to split Aces, and to balance this advantage the player is allowed to draw only one card to each Ace and may not double down. An Ace and a 10-value made after splitting is not counted as Blackjack. It pays 1 to 1, not 3 to 2, and ties with dealer's 21.

(b) In some casinos a third card of the same kind, if drawn immediately to one of the two cards, may be split again, to form three, or even four, separate hands; but Aces may not be split in this way.

(c) Few casinos allow a double after a split but in some casinos a player who has split any card other than Aces is allowed to play the hands with all the normal options: he may double after his second card and may be hit more than once.

The strategy for splitting pairs

Pair splitting, like doubling down, is optional. Assuming the rules set out in the last paragraph, this is the recommended play:

(a) Always split Aces, despite the limitations that follow.

(b) Never split 10-10; it is better to play the hand as a pat 20.

(c) Split 9-9 against 2 to 6 and 8 or 9, but not against 10 or Ace. You don't split against 7 because you can play the hand as a pat 18 against dealer's quite likely 17.

(d) Always split 8-8. This is not because 8 is a particularly good card, but because otherwise you will have to play from 16, a wretched number.

(e) Split 7-7 when dealer shows 2 to 8. You are not favored when dealer shows 7 or 8, but you have a better chance than if you play from 14.

(f) Split 6-6 against 2 to 7.

(g) Never split 5-5. You do better to draw to 10.

(h) Split 4-4 only against a 5.

(i) Split 3-3 and 2-2 against dealer's 2 to 7.

This diagram shows the full strategy:

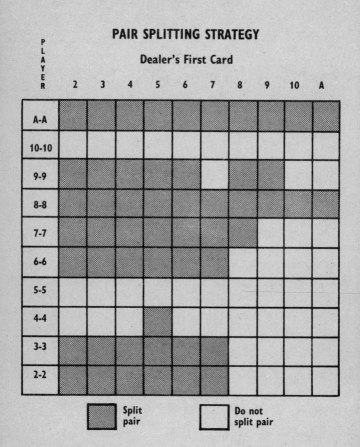

PAIR SPLITTING STRATEGY

Dealer's First Card

Split pair / Do not split pair

Once again, the best way to remember this strategy is to understand the logic behind it. Until you have mastered the basic technique of Blackjack and so can give your full attention to minutiae, you will be giving very little away if you simplify as follows: **Always split A-A and 8-8; don't split 10-10 5-5 or 4-4; split other pairs only when the dealer's card is for him a relatively poor one (usually 2 to 7).**

Insurance strategy

As mentioned earlier, when dealer's face-up card is an Ace you can insure against his drawing a 10-value and making Blackjack. You get odds of 2 to 1, but as the true odds, other things being equal, are 9 to 4, the only time when insurance may be a good proposition is when the proportion of 10-value cards remaining in the deck is unusually high. (Most dealers will tell you that insurance favors the casino and should only be taken if player has an excellent hand.) In this case the expectation of the dealer making Blackjack may become less than 2 to 1 against. To know when this situation has arisen, you will need to count the cards, using the method described in the next section.

5. Counting and Advanced Strategy

In the early days of Blackjack only a single deck was used and every card was dealt except the first and last. It was possible for a professional player to assess very accurately the composition of the last few cards and many opportunities were presented. Some casinos protect themselves nowadays by using more than one deck and suspending play long before the end. (Most casinos use four decks.) Thus only general tendencies can be observed, but these tendencies are still worth studying.

The importance of 10s and 5s

Broadly speaking, 10s in the deck are good cards for the player. They improve his chances of buying a good card when he has doubled down and they increase the dealer's chances of going bust when, by the rules, he is obliged to draw to totals between 12 and 16.

5s, on the other hand, are bad cards for you and therefore good cards for the dealer. He is now less likely to break when drawing to totals between 12 and 16.

Counting the 10s and 5s

Suppose you are playing in a game where only two decks are used and cards are dealt face up, so that you have time to make certain observations. Half-way through, your observations may tell you that the remainder of the deck is 10-rich or 10-poor, 5-rich or 5-poor. The normal expectation, after 52 cards have been played, is that sixteen 10-value cards and four 5s should have appeared, and that the same number should be left in the second half of the deck. But if you have observed, say, only eleven 10s and six 5s you know that the remainder of the deck will be 10-rich (good for you) and 5-poor (good for you). You may now assume that the weather is favorable and you may increase your normal wager, perhaps to a dramatic extent, almost from minimum to maximum. The composition of the deck may also alter your playing strategy. For example, if a high proportion of 5s is left towards the end of the deck you may decide to draw to a stiff (12 to 16) when the dealer has a low card. Certainly the advantage of counting 10s and 5s is small, but many serious players consider it worth the attempt.

Counting all high and low cards

Though the most important, 10s and 5s are not the only cards worth noting. The accuracy of your calculations will be increased if you take note of all the high and low cards. This is not so difficult as it may seem.

Whenever a low card (2 to 6) appears, count plus 1. Ignore cards with a value of 7 8 and 9. Count minus 1 for 10 and Ace. Using this reckoning, there are five low cards and five high ones (four 10s and the Ace). If at any time your number is a substantial plus, the remainder of the deck should favor you, because now relatively few low cards (good for the dealer) are left but a high proportion of 10s and Aces (good for you). So now you strike, increasing your stake and altering your strategy. If very few low cards are left it may be sensible on occasions to stand on 15 or 16 against dealer's high card.

A simple way to estimate 10s

After a time the basic playing strategy in Blackjack becomes automatic, requiring no concentration. When you reach that stage you will be ready to adopt more advanced strategies. Begin by taking note of the 10-value cards. It is not necessary to count them one by one and relate them to the number of cards played. Remember simply that the average proportion is 4 in 13. Observe each group of 8 or 12 cards and note how many 10s appear. If the ratio falls below 1 in 4 you have a situation where the rest of the deck is 10-rich (good for you).

The casino advantage in Blackjack

The casino's advantage in Blackjack is estimated at about 6%, but this depends to some extent on how well the customers play. Many players make consistent errors in basic situations, the commonest being a reluctance to be hit with 15 or 16 when the dealer has a high card. A player whose basic strategy is accurate and who adopts the methods described in this section, altering both stakes and tactics at the right moment, has a good chance to come out ahead.

The casinos claim that in play with proper basic strategy the house advantage is only $\frac{1}{2}$ of 1%.

"Surrendering"

Some casinos offer a "surrender clause." A player, after receiving his first two cards, may opt to drop out of that particular deal and lose only half of his bet.

Tipping

Players who have been winning many hands (either by getting Blackjack or because the dealer has busted) give tips to the dealer either by handing him chips or by placing chips at the edge of the box (in front of his own wager) to play with the next hand. If the player wins the next hand, his tip money is paid even money (dealer then takes it as his tip) and if player loses the hand, the tip money goes to the casino with the regular bet. Dealers usually share their tips with other dealers.

Craps

CRAPS

1. Nature of the Game

In Craps a customer throws two six-sided dice, which must traverse the length of the table, striking the rubber perimeter before they settle. A wide variety of bets can be made on the results of single or successive throws. While the casino, naturally, never gives the customer the opportunity to make a bet which is in his favor, there are some situations where the house advantage is nil. The customer cannot bet on these situations exclusively, but by good management he can play for a long period with very small odds against him. Since the casino's advantage on different types of bet ranges from over 16% to less than 1%, it is highly important to know the odds on various betting options.

Layout of the table

A Crap layout usually has three sections. The two outside sections are identical, so customers can stand at either end of the table. All can wager on the so-called Proposition Bets in the center of the layout.

Layout of the Craps Table

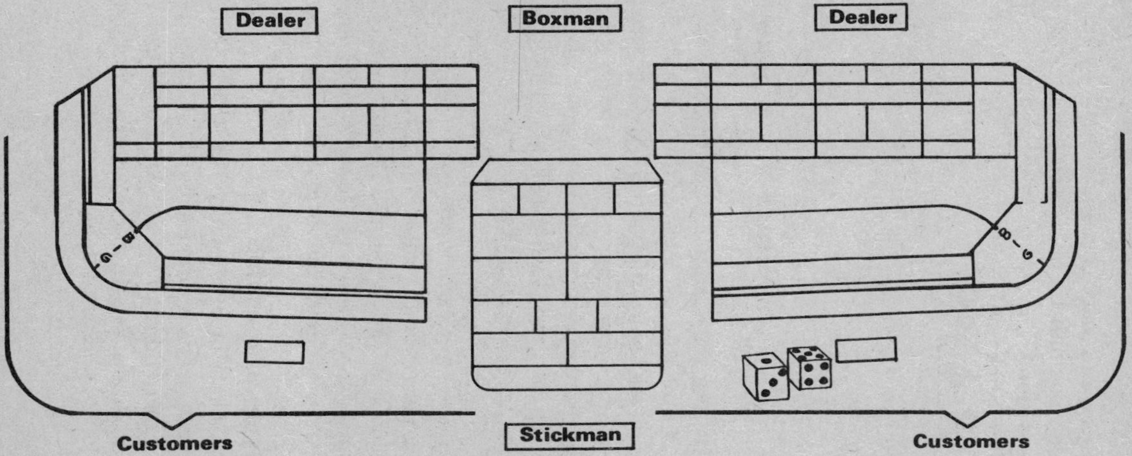

Dealer

Boxman

Dealer

Stickman

Customers

Customers

The Dealers give change, collect losing bets, pay out winners, and place bets on request.

The Boxman handles currency and exercises general supervision.

The Stickman is responsible for the handling of the dice and for placing the Proposition Bets in the center section.

The layout of the table (and, indeed, the whole procedure in Craps) is confusing at first acquaintance. If you are not familiar with the game you will need to refer frequently to the illustration on page 40.

Scene at the Craps Table

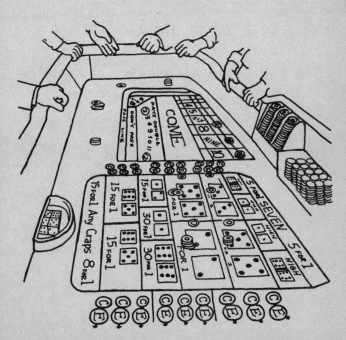

Craps Table

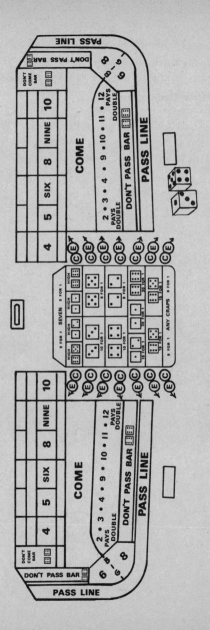

The meaning of the mysterious terms illustrated in the diagram will become clear as we proceed.

How the game begins

Assume that you are the first player at the table. You stand at one end of the long table and the Stickman will offer you a selection of dice, from which you choose two. You throw them past the Stickman with sufficient force to bounce against the barrier at the opposite end. As the "shooter," you must wager on either the Pass Line Bet or Don't Pass, described in the next section. You will continue until a 7 appears on a Point Roll; again, see the next section for a description of this occurrence.

2. The Four Basic Wagers
(Pass Line, Don't Pass, Come, Don't Come)

Come-out roll

The first roll of the dice is called the Come-out roll. There is a new Come-out roll whenever a Point has been made (see below), or when there is a decision on the Come-out roll (2, 3, 12, 7 or 11).

Pass Line Bet

This is the most popular bet in Craps, though not, from the customer's angle, the most advantageous. It operates in two stages. You place your bet in the area marked PASS LINE, which runs round the outside, above the level of the playing surface. Then:

First stage:

(a) If the dice thrown in the Come-out roll total 7 or 11, called a Natural, you win and are paid 1 to 1.

(b) If the Come-out roll totals 2 3 or 12, called a Crap, you have lost your stake.

(c) If the Come-out roll results in 4 5 6 8 9 or 10 you are still in the game and your fate will depend on subsequent rolls. These six numbers are called Points. You will note that they are indicated in the layout above COME, with SIX and NINE spelt out. When a Point has been established, the dealer will place a round Point marker in the appropriate box. Then the second stage begins.

When you have made a Pass Line Bet you are more likely to win than lose on the opening throw. Remember that you win when a natural 7 or 11 is thrown, lose when Crap 2 3 or 12 appears. The number 7 can turn up in six ways (6–1, 1–6, 5–2, 2–5, 4–3, 3–4), 11 in two ways (6–5, 5–6). The total frequency for the Crap numbers is only four (1–1, 1–2, 2–1, 6–6), so you are twice as likely (8 chances to 4) to win as lose. Remember, however, that if a Point number appears (24 possibilities) your money is still at risk, and from now on the odds turn sharply against you.

Second stage :

A Point has been established—either 4 5 6 8 9 or 10. Now you lose if 7 turns up before your Point. You win if your Point turns up before 7. The shooter will continue to throw until either 7 or the Point number appears. As 7 has a greater frequency than any of the other Points, you are a non-favorite at this stage, though to different degrees: with 6 or 8, for example, you have a better chance than with 4 or 10.

This diagram summarizes the Pass Bet rules:

PASS BET RULES

Come-out Roll
Natural 7 or 11 — WIN
Crap 2, 3 or 12 — LOSE

POINTS

4	5	6	8	9	10

Point Rolls
Point — WIN
7 — LOSE

In short, **you win at once when 7 or 11 appears, lose to 2 3 or 12; when a Point is thrown (4 5 6 8 9 or 10) you want your Point to be thrown again before 7.**

The house advantage on a Pass Line Bet is 1.414%. It is often possible, as will appear later when we discuss Odds Bets, to follow the Pass Line Bet with further wagers where the house has no advantage, so that the customer's disadvantage may be spread over a bigger investment.

Before reading on, be absolutely sure that you understand the operation of a Pass Line Bet and that you know what is meant by the terms Come-out roll, Natural, Crap, and Point.

Don't Pass Bet

As an alternative to betting on Pass, the customer can bet on Don't Pass, placing his money on the Don't Pass Bar. Don't Pass is the opposite, the mirror image, of Pass, but not the *exact* opposite, because if that were the case the customer would have the advantage, obviously.

First stage:

In the Pass Line Bet, natural 7 or 11 win for the customer, crap 2 3 or 12 lose. In Don't Pass 7 or 11 lose, crap 2 and 3 will win, crap 12 is a "push," neither winning nor losing, and the casino advantage arises from this one circumstance. As before, the numbers 4 5 6 8 9 and 10 constitute a Point.

You may note that on the Don't Pass Bar there is a representation of 6–6, the "barred" number which produces a tie when thrown on the Come-out roll. In some casinos the barred number is 2, which has the same frequency (1–1 instead of 6–6). In others the barred number is 3; this is disadvantageous to the player, because 3 can turn up in two ways (2–1 or 1–2).

Second stage:

When a Point has been established, the rules are the exact opposite to those of Pass Line: you win if 7 turns up before the Point, lose if the Point is thrown before 7.

Betting Don't Pass, **you lose at once when 7 or 11 appears, win when 2 or 3 appears, tie when 12 appears; when a Point is thrown you want 7 to be thrown before your Point.**

It will be readily understood that whereas in Pass you are favored at the first stage, non-favored at the second stage, in Don't Pass it is the other way around.

This diagram illustrates the Don't Pass rules:

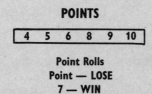

DON'T PASS BETS

Come-out Roll
Natural 7 or 11 — LOSE
Crap 2 or 3 — WIN
Crap 12 — PUSH

POINTS

4	5	6	8	9	10

Point Rolls
Point — LOSE
7 — WIN

The house advantage on Don't Pass is 1.402%, fractionally less than for Pass Line. Again, it is often possible to follow with bets where the house has no advantage.

Losing the dice

One further point must be mentioned before we leave the Pass and Don't Pass bets: the shooter retains the dice until he throws a 7 on a Point roll. When this happens (or earlier if the shooter wishes) the Stickman will offer the dice to the next player, moving around the table in clockwise direction.

Come Bet

Whereas the Pass and Don't Pass bets are made only on the Come-out roll, a Come Bet is placed only when a Point has been established. A Come Bet is placed on the surface marked Come, at the shooter's end usually, but a player at the other end can make a Come Bet even if it gets in the way of the dice.

The Come Bet always wins and loses according to the same rules as Pass. At first, natural 7 or 11 win for the customer, crap 2 3 and 12 lose. When a new Point is established by the throw of 4 5 6 8 9 or 10, the Come Bet is moved to the appropriate box. The bet wins when this Point appears again before a 7, loses if a 7 appears first.

For example, suppose that as a result of the Come-out roll 9 becomes the Pass Line Point. A Come Bet is placed and one of the Point numbers appears, such as 4. Now 4 is the Come Point and the fortunes of the bet depend on whether 7 is thrown before 4 (losing) or 4 before 7 (winning).

When a wager in the Come Point wins, the dealer pays it off on a 1–1 basis and places all the proceeds in the Come area. Unless removed, it remains as the player's next bet.

A Come Bet is essentially the same as a Pass Bet, operating with a different Point number. The house advantage is therefore the same, 1.414%.

Don't Come Bet

Just as Don't Pass is in all respects except one (the barred point, usually 12) the opposite of Pass, so Don't Come is the opposite of Come, with the same exception.

Don't Come bets are placed in the Don't Come area, which at one end of the table is on the left of Point 4, at the other end on the right of Point 10. The bet is made only when a Pass Line Point has been established. The rules are the same as for Don't Pass. Immediate 7 or 11 lose, Crap 2 and 3 win, 12 is a push. When one of the Point numbers turns up, the wager is placed in the appropriate box and the rules are now the opposite of a Come Bet: you want 7 to turn up before your Don't Come Point Number. When your bet wins, the proceeds are placed in the Don't Come Box and become your next wager unless removed.

Since Don't Come depends on the same chances as Don't Pass, the house advantage is the same 1.402%.

Summary of Pass, Don't Pass, Come, Don't Come

The very similarity between these standard bets makes it difficult at first to remember which is which, so we do not hesitate to repeat the main features again here:

Pass Line Bet wins at once when natural 7 or 11 is thrown, loses when Crap 2 3 or 12 appears. When a Point (4 5 6 8 9 or 10) is established, the player loses when 7 turns up before his Point, wins when his Point is thrown before 7.

Don't Pass is the reverse except in one particular. It loses at once when natural 7 or 11 is thrown, wins when Crap 2 or 3 appears, ties when 12 appears (the exception). When a Point has been established, the bet wins when 7 is thrown before the Point, loses when the Point is thrown first.

Come Bet is made only when a Pass Line Point has been established. The rules then are the same as for Pass Line: win on 7 or 11, lose on Crap 2 3 or 12; if a Point is thrown, player wants the Point to be repeated before 7.

Don't Come Bet similarly is made only when a Pass Line Point has been established. The rules are then the same as for Don't Pass: lose on 7 or 11, win on Crap 2 and 3, tie on 12; if a Point is thrown, player wants 7 to appear before the Point.

3. Odds Bets

The Odds Bet is the one bet that offers no casino advantage. Opportunity to make an Odds Bet occurs only when the customer has invested in one of the four standard bets already described—Pass, Don't Pass, Come and Don't Come. When a Point has been established, the player who made the original bet waits to see whether his Point will turn up before or after a 7. At this stage the Odds Bet permits him to reinforce his bet. The chances vary according to the nature of the bet and the number of the Point, but in all cases the casino pays off at the fair mathematical odds.

An Odds Bet on Pass or Come

Suppose you have invested in a Pass Line Bet and Point 5 is established. You may now place an additional wager for the same amount or much more behind your Pass Line Bet, signifying that you want to make an Odds Bet on 5. If 7 turns up before 5 you lose both bets. If 5 turns up before 7 you win both bets. You are paid off at 1–1 for your Pass Line bet but receive the full odds of 3 to 2 in respect of your Odds Bet. This is the right odds because 7 can be thrown in 6 ways, 5 in only 4 ways.

An Odds Bet on a Come Point is exactly the same. You identify the Point to the dealer, saying, for example, "Odds on 10." He will place your Odds Bet on top of your Come wager. Again, the Odds Bet and the Come Bet will be paid off at different odds. Your Odds Bet will pay 2 to 1 now, since there are only 3 ways of throwing 10 (6–4, 4–6 and 5–5). All chips (the original wagers and the pay-offs) will be moved to Come for the next roll and will remain there unless removed by the player.

When a Come-out roll intervenes

When the player's Come Point and the Pass Line Point established by the shooter are different, it may happen that the Pass Line Point will turn up and a Come-out roll will follow. In this case the Come Bet is still operative but the Odds Bet is "off" unless the player specifies to the dealer that his wagers "work" on the Come-out roll.

The payout for an Odds Bet

The payout for an Odds Bet, as we have indicated, reflects the likelihood of the Point being thrown as compared with 7 being thrown. The payouts are shown here:

ODDS RATIOS

Total		Payoff		Totals
7	=	6 to 3	=	4 or 10
7	=	6 to 4	=	5 or 9
7	=	6 to 5	=	6 or 8

There are 3 ways of throwing 4 or 10, so the customer receives 6 to 3 for his money; 4 ways of throwing 5 or 9, so he receives 6 to 4; 5 ways of throwing 6 or 8, so he receives 6 to 5.

Maximizing the Odds

A casino will normally not pay out fractions of the minimum unit. For example, if the minimum is $1 the casino will not pay out $1.50. To a limited extent, the customer can exploit this tendency and in certain situations make an Odds Bet for a slightly larger amount than the original stake. This is known as obtaining Full Odds.

The best amount to invest for this purpose is 3 units of the minimum stake at the table. Suppose that Point 4 or 10 is established. In this event there is no gain: just 3 units can be invested at Odds of 2 to 1. If the Point is 5 or 9, the player can make an Odds Bet, not of $4\frac{1}{2}$ to 3, but of 6 to 4. In other words, he is able to invest more on the Odds Bet than on the original wager. And if 6 or 8 turns up, justifying odds of 6 to 5, the player is able to invest 5 units to win 6. This table expresses the Full Odds:

FULL ODDS

Dice	Payoff	Amount of Odds Bet
4 or 10	2 to 1	Equals amount of flat wager
5 or 9	3 to 2	Next even amount of chips
6 or 8	6 to 5	Nearest multiple of 5 chips

While 3 units is the amount that leads to the biggest proportionate increase, a similar advance is possible with most sums.

A few casinos allow Double Odds. This means that a player can make an Odds Bet of twice as much as his original bet, provided no fractions are involved. One way to take advantage of this concession is to make an original wager in units of 4. Then the Odds Bet can always be double the original amount, the highest being 8 Odds on 4 Points. Some casinos allow Odds of 10 by giving 2.5 times on bets of 4 units.

An original wager of 3 chips enables you to take the fullest advantage of the single Odds Bet on Don't Pass and Don't Come. The reason appears in the illustration on the opposite page.

MAXIMIZING FULL ODDS for DON'T BETS

Flat Wager = 1 Chip

Odds Wager	Totals	Payoff
2 Chips	4 or 10	1 to 2
3 Chips	5 or 9	2 to 3
0 Chips	6 or 8	0

Flat Wager = 3 Chips

Odds Wager	Totals	Payoff
6 Chips	4 or 10	3 to 6
6 Chips	5 or 9	4 to 6
6 Chips	6 or 8	5 to 6

A player who has invested a "flat wager" of 1 chip cannot lay the odds on 6 or 8 because he would not be allowed to invest 6 chips at this point, to win 5. But a player who has made a flat wager of 3 chips can now invest 6 chips on all three propositions, obtaining full odds in each case.

Are Odds Bets advantageous?

You will sometimes hear the following argument:

"Odds Bets are an illusion—just a casino trick. Since you are getting the true odds on all bets of this kind, you will be just as well off if you never make an Odds Bet."

That is true in a way, but from the player's angle the advantage of betting Odds is that he incurs a smaller disadvantage on the total he invests. If you bet Don't Pass and follow with an Odds Bet at full odds when a Point has been thrown, your disadvantage in relation to the amount you have invested is only 0.80%. Apart from very occasional situations that may arise in Blackjack or in French Baccarat, this is the best proposition you will ever find in a casino.

4. Optimum Strategy in Craps

We have reached an important point now in our discussion of tactics in Craps, because we have covered all the most advantageous wagers. Many other types of wager are available, but they are inferior to the strategies we have described, most of them very much inferior.

This is the suggested course of action for a newcomer to the game:

(1) Begin by making the Pass Line wager only.

(2) When comfortable with this, bet full odds on the Point rolls.

(3) Wager on the Come Bets and bet full odds on the Point rolls.

These are alternatives:

(4) Make a Don't Pass wager and lay full odds.

(5) Make a Don't Come wager and lay full odds.

Bear in mind that the house advantage in Pass, Come, Don't Pass and Don't Come is in all cases less than $1\frac{1}{2}\%$ and that even this advantage is reduced by taking or laying full odds.

5. The Remaining Bets

There are many ways of losing your money quickly at Craps. If you study this very important table showing the house advantage for various types of bet, you will see how unprofitable most of them are.

CASINO ADVANTAGE

DO's

Pass	1.414%
Come	1.414%
Place 6 or 8	1.515%
Place 5 or 9	4.000%
Place 4 or 10	6.667%

DON'Ts

Don't Pass	1.402%
Don't Come	1.402%
Lay 4 or 10	2.439%
Lay 5 or 9	3.225%
Lay 6 or 8	4.000%

PROPOSITIONS

Field (20 to 19)	2.778%
Field (20 to 18)	5.556%
Big 6 or Big 8	9.091%
Hard 6 or Hard 8	9.091%
Hard 4 or Hard 10	11.111%
Any Craps	11.111%
3 or 11 (15 to 1)	11.111%
3 or 11 (14 to 1)	16.667%
2 or 12 (30 to 1)	13.889%
2 or 12 (29 to 1)	16.667%
7	16.667%

One-Roll Propositions

We turn now to "proposition bets," which are placed by the Stickman on the area in front of him between the two outside sections. It looks like this:

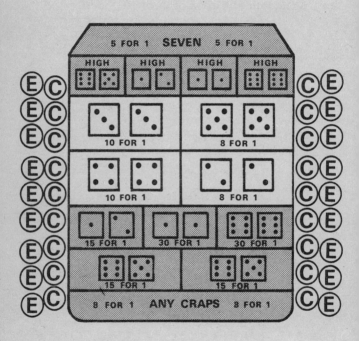

Observe the top line, reading SEVEN 5 for 1. This means that the player can back 7 and receive 5 chips if it wins. He is getting odds of 4 to 1 instead of the true 5 to 1.

In the lower half of the layout you will see 15 for 1 for 2–1 and 6–5. This represents odds of 14 to 1 instead of the true 17 to 1. Then for 1–1 or 6–6 you receive 30 for

1, which represents odds of 29 to 1 instead of the true 35 to 1. Some casinos are a point more generous for these wagers. Finally, the bottom line, 8 for 1 Any Craps means that you receive 7 to 1 for the numbers 2 3 and 12 combined instead of the true 8 to 1.

The other symbols on this layout refer to other wagers, described below.

Horn Bet

This is a combination of Any Craps (2 3 and 12) and 11. In the layout shown here the chips would be placed at the junction of Any Craps and 6–5. The bet must be made in units of 4, so that the winning combination can be paid off at the odds shown, less the chips lost on the other wagers.

A Horn High bet, made beneath the word High on the proposition layout, is a 5-unit bet, consisting of 1 unit on 3 numbers and 2 units on the fourth. The payoff is on the same principle, the customer doing best when the number on which he has 2 units is successful.

Hop Bets

Hop Bets are one-roll wagers similar to the one-roll proposition bets. They are laid by the Boxman. Depending on the rules of the casino, it may be possible to invest on any of the combinations that can be thrown (there are 21 such combinations). The odds for any *double*, such as 3–3, are the standard 29 to 1; for any *odd* combination, such as 5 and 4 (which can be thrown in two ways), 14 to 1.

Hardway Propositions

The dice combinations shown in the center of the proposition layout, 3-3 5-5 4-4 and 2-2, represent the ways in which the four even-numbered Point totals can be thrown by means of a double. A stake placed on one of these is a wager that the double will turn up before either a 7 is thrown or the total of the Point is thrown by way of two odd numbers. Thus if you place your money on 4-4 you win only if 4-4 turns up before 7 or 6-2 or 5-3. In this example 6-2 and 5-3 are known as the "easy" way to throw 8, while 4-4 is the "hard" way.

The large figures indicate the odds: 10 for 1 (9 to 1 against) when you back 3-3 or 4-4, 8 for 1 (7 to 1 against) when you back 5-5 or 2-2. The odds for 3-3 and 4-4 are higher than for 4 and 10 because there are two "easy" combinations making up 6 and 8, only one making up 4 and 10. A bet on hard 6 or hard 8 is slightly better than on hard 4 or hard 10, but the difference is unimportant because all wagers on the proposition layout are disastrous for the player.

Since we do not recommend their adoption, we will describe the less attractive bets quite briefly, without going into details of where they are placed and how winnings are collected. A dealer will always be ready to explain.

Buy Bets

A Buy Bet may be made on any Point. It wins when the Point appears before 7. Payment is the same as for an Odds Bet except that the casino charges 5% commission. The weight of this deduction is least when the wager is for 20 chips and an additional chip is deducted for commission.

Lay Bets

Lay Bets are the opposite of Buy Bets. Like Don't Pass, they win on 7 and lose when the Point appears. The customer is therefore betting with odds against him. Suppose he makes a Lay Bet on Point 4 or Point 10: he will lay 40 to win 20 and the 5% commission will be payable on the winnings, not the total invested. This makes Lay Bets somewhat more favorable to the customer than Buy Bets.

Place Bets

A Place Bet can be made on any Point or any combination of Points on any roll. The bet wins or loses in the same way as the Buy Bet. Payoffs are based on the true odds ratio plus a 1 to 1 wager which is advantageous to the casino. Thus instead of 8 to 4 on Points 4 or 10 the odds paid are 9 to 5; instead of 6 to 4 on Points 5 or 9, 7 to 5; and instead of 6 to 5 on Points 6 or 8, 7 to 6. This last wager has only a 1.515 advantage for the house and is the best proposition available after the Do and Don't bets.

Big 6 or Big 8

At the corners of the layout you will see the signs Big 6 and Big 8. You can bet either of these to occur before a 7 is thrown. Since 7 can be thrown in 6 ways, 6 and 8 in only 5 ways, the wager is clearly imprudent.

Field Bet

A player making a Field Bet backs the seven totals in the foreground of the layout, 2 3 4 9 10 11 and 12, against the four center numbers, 5 6 7 8. As the frequency of the center numbers is 20 against 16 for the Field, the numbers 2 and 12 (to reduce the house advantage) pay 2 to 1 instead of 1 to 1, and in some casinos the odds are further equated by paying 3 to 1 on either 2 or 12.

KENO

1. Nature of the Game

Keno is a "numbers" game. In the Keno lounge, or elsewhere in the casino, players can obtain tickets which look like the one on page 59.

As seen on page 62, the ticket has 80 numbers. The customer selects from 1 to 15 numbers on which to wager. Then the casino, with the aid of a contrivance that blows 20 out of 80 balls into a special compartment, makes a random choice of 20 numbers. The customer wins when a sufficient proportion of the numbers he has marked coincide with those chosen at random by the casino. These numbers are shown in various parts of the casino on an electrical board.

Keno as a gambling medium

As a medium for serious gamblers, Keno is a non-starter. It is possible to place bets in a great variety of ways, but the house advantage is always close to 28%. Like the football pools in Britain, Lotto in Germany, and the *tiercé* on racing in France, the game is popular because it is possible to win large sums for a small outlay. Also, the game is leisurely as compared with the rat-a-tat of American roulette, not to mention the justly named one-armed bandits, or slot machines. Thus the customer, though operating at very poor odds, will not lose his money so quickly as at the other pastimes.

2. Making Simple Bets

Marking a ticket

Having obtained his ticket from a Keno desk or counter, the customer marks his selections with a black crayon by placing an X over the numbers of his choice.

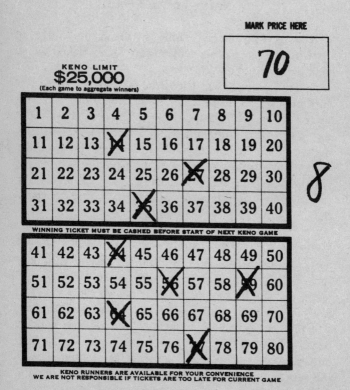

He may select from 1 to 15 numbers. Supposing that he marks 8 numbers, his completed ticket may look like the example opposite.

The figure 8, confirming the number of choices, is written on the right. The figure 70 in the price slot indicates that the player proposes to wager 70 cents. (This may or may not be the minimum in your casino, but let's use it as our example.) Dollar signs and decimal points are not used. When the price is over $1 the cents are written above a line, as will be seen in later diagrams.

The customer hands his ticket to a Keno runner, who is at the disposal of patrons not in the Keno lounge, or directly to a Keno writer, who will issue a duplicate, retaining the original.

The payoff

The casino will provide a brochure containing details of the payoff for all standard bets and numerous "specials." This diagram shows the payoff for various degrees of success when the player has marked (a) 4 numbers, and (b) 8 numbers, betting in units of 70 cents:

PAYOFF SCHEDULE

MARK 4 SPOTS

Catch	Play 70c	Play $1.40	Play $3.50
2 Pays	70c	$1.40	$3.50
3 Pays	$2.70	5.40	13.50
4 Pays	80.00	160.00	400.00

MARK 8 SPOTS

Catch	Play 70c	Play $1.40	Play $3.50
5 Pays	$6.00	$12.00	$30.00
6 Pays	60.00	120.00	300.00
7 Pays	1,150.00	2,300.00	5,750.00
8 Pays	12,500.00	25,000.00	25,000.00

A player who has marked 4 numbers gets his money back when he has 2 "catches"; that is, when two of the numbers he has marked are among the 20 selected at random by the casino. A player who has marked 8 numbers needs 5 catches to be a winner. A player who has invested $1.40 stands to win the maximum of $25,000 if all 8 numbers are caught in the net. This win, however, is somewhat theoretical, because this is the maximum that the casino is allowed by law to pay out for a single game. Thus big winners may not receive the full amount that would otherwise be due them according to the schedule.

When the player judges that he is entitled to a payout he takes (or dispatches) his ticket to one of the Keno windows, where the ticket will be checked and paid. This must be done before the next game commences. Big wins have to be reported to the government and may eventually be subject to tax.

3. Way and Combination Bets

The majority of Keno players do not bet only on single numbers but combine groups of numbers in various ways. A typical "combination" entry is shown on the opposite page.

It will be observed that certain groups of numbers are circled. There are three such groups, each containing 4 "spots."

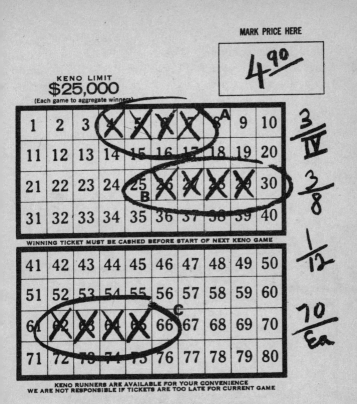

A Keno Combination Entry

The numerals in the margin indicate how the groups are combined to produce several wagers. This is called "conditioning" the bet. The first figure, $\frac{3}{IV}$, signifies that the player wishes to combine the three groups of four with one another to produce 3 4-spot entries, the groups A B and C. (In accordance with custom, the numerals 3 to 5 are written in Roman figures.) Secondly, the player has written $\frac{3}{8}$, indicating that he wishes to make 3 8-spot entries. These will be the numbers represented by group A plus group B, A plus C, and B plus C. Finally, the player joins all three groups in a 12-spot entry, shown as $\frac{1}{12}$. He has made 7 entries (3 of 4, 3 of 8, 1 of 12), so the cost of the ticket at 70 cents a time is $4.90, marked in the top corner.

This next example contains 8 circles, each with 3 spots:

The ticket can be conditioned in various ways. It would be possible to create:

(a) 8 3-spot tickets (the 8 circles).

(b) 28 combinations of two circles each, 6 spots.

(c) 56 combinations of 3 circles, 9 spots.

(d) 70 combinations of 4 circles, 12 spots.

(e) 56 combinations of 5 circles, 15 spots.

This is the limit, because a combination of 6 circles would involve an entry containing 18 spots, which is above the maximum of 15.

On the present occasion the player has chosen to invest on (b) and (e). He has invested $1.40 each in respect of the 28 combinations making up (b), and 70 cents each on the 56 combinations making up (e). The letter W stands for Way. Each part of the bet totals $39.20, so the price of the ticket is $78.40.

How to assess the number of combinations

You may wonder how long it takes to work out the fact that in the example above groups of 3 circles can be combined in 56 ways, groups of 4 circles in 70 ways. The calculation can be made in a few seconds.

Take the first situation, where there are 8 circles and you want to combine them in groups of 3. Starting at the "long" end (the number of circles), multiply 8 x 7 x 6, stopping after three digits since you are dealing with groups of 3. Divide that figure by 1 x 2 x 3, again stopping after three digits.

Apply the same method to the problem of combining 4 groups. Again start at the long end and multiply 8 x 7 x 6 x 5, stopping after four digits as there are 4 groups. Divide by 1 x 2 x 3 x 4.

When the circles contain different numbers of spots

This ticket appears to be more complicated, because the circles contain different numbers of spots:

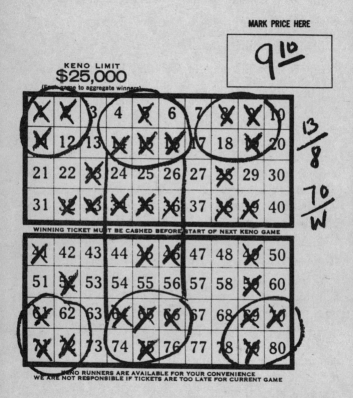

Here there are 4 groups of 3 spots, circled, 2 groups of 4 spots, circled, and 3 of 5 spots, conventionally enclosed between lines.

The player making out the ticket has written $\frac{13}{8}$, so he has concentrated on combinations of 8 spots. When a ticket is conditioned it must cover all combinations that make up the indicated total, since otherwise there would be ambiguity. (Normally, the Keno writer will note any inaccuracy in the conditioning.) Do you see the 13 combinations of 8? First, there are 3 groups of 5, which can be mixed with 4 groups of 3 to provide 8-spot entries. Multiply the group totals, 4 x 3, and you have the answer — 12 possibilities. Also, there are the two groups of 4. So the total of combinations containing 8 spots is 13 and the cost of the ticket, at 70 cents for each wager, is $9.10.

A King ticket

Finally, a ticket may have one or more circles containing only 1 spot. This is called a King ticket. (See following two pages.)

If it were not for the circle on number 39 on the first ticket this would be a simple 9-spot ticket. As it stands, it has been conditioned in two ways: a 9-spot entry and an 8-spot entry, not containing the number in the circle.

On the second ticket, an unusual example, all 5 spots have been circled as King spots.

The ticket has been conditioned in every possible way—5 1-spot entries, 10 2-spots (note that "one" and "two" are written out in this context), 10 3-spot entries, 5 4-spot entries, and 1 5-spot entry. There are 31 entries, so the price at 70 cents each is $21.70.

140

KENO LIMIT
$25,000
(Each game to aggregate winners)

1	2	3	4	5	X	7	8	9	10
11	12	13	14	15	16	17	X8	19	20
21	X2	X3	24	25	26	27	28	29	30
31	32	33	34	X5	36	37	38	(X9)	40

1/8

1/9

WINNING TICKET MUST BE CASHED BEFORE START OF NEXT KENO GAME

70/EA

41	42	43	44	45	46	47	48	49	50
51	X2	53	54	55	56	X7	58	59	60
61	62	63	64	65	66	67	68	69	70
71	72	73	74	75	X6	77	78	79	80

KENO RUNNERS ARE AVAILABLE FOR YOUR CONVENIENCE
WE ARE NOT RESPONSIBLE IF TICKETS ARE TOO LATE FOR CURRENT GAME

A King Ticket with a 9-Spot Entry and an 8-Spot Entry

21 70

KENO LIMIT
$25,000
(Each game to aggregate winners)

1	2	3	(4)	5	6	7	8	9	10
11	12	13	14	15	16	(17)	18	19	20
21	22	23	24	25	26	27	28	29	30
31	32	33	(34)	35	36	37	38	39	40

WINNING TICKET MUST BE CASHED BEFORE START OF NEXT KENO GAME

41	42	43	44	45	46	47	48	49	50
51	52	53	54	55	56	(57)	58	59	60
61	62	(63)	64	65	66	67	68	69	70
71	72	73	74	75	76	77	78	79	80

$\frac{5}{\text{ONE}}$

$\frac{10}{\text{TWO}}$

$\frac{10}{\text{III}}$

$\frac{5}{\text{IV}}$

$\frac{\text{}}{\text{V}}$

$\frac{70}{\text{EA}}$

KENO RUNNERS ARE AVAILABLE FOR YOUR CONVENIENCE
WE ARE NOT RESPONSIBLE IF TICKETS ARE TOO LATE FOR CURRENT GAME

A Ticket with 5 King Spots for a Total of 31 Entries

Baccarat

BACCARAT

1. Nature of the Game

The game described as Baccarat (the *t* is silent) in America is not quite the same as Baccarat in France. The American form of the game is known in Britain and elsewhere as Punto Banco.

Baccarat (French style), Baccarat (American style), and Chemin-de-fer are essentially the same simple game. The differences lie in who plays against whom, and who handles the cards.

Object of the game

The two sides, Bank and Player, are given two cards to begin with and may in some circumstances take a third card. The object is to attain the highest pip total. As the first digit is not counted, the highest number is 9.

Value of cards

As in Blackjack, any Ten, Jack, Queen or King counts as 10, which in this game means zero. Ace counts as 1. Other cards have their normal pip value

Layout of the Baccarat Table

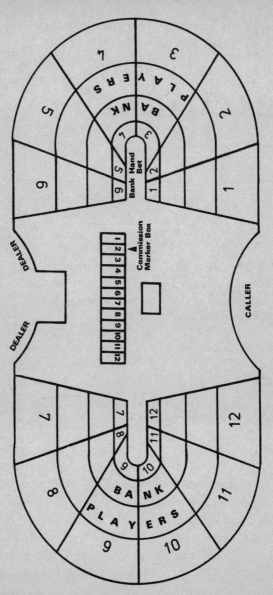

and the different suits have no significance. The diagram below shows how hand totals are counted.

VALUE OF CARDS

$$\boxed{2} + \boxed{3} = \boxed{5} \qquad \boxed{2} + \boxed{1} + \boxed{4} = \boxed{7}$$

$$\boxed{0} + \boxed{9} = \boxed{9} \qquad \boxed{0} + \boxed{3} + \boxed{7} = \boxed{10}$$

$$\boxed{8} + \boxed{9} = \boxed{17} \qquad \boxed{8} + \boxed{3} + \boxed{5} = \boxed{16}$$

The two stages of play

Assume that two players, A and B, are playing a hand against one another. A gives a card to B and a card to himself, then a second card to each. If either player has a pat 8 or 9, no more cards are drawn. Otherwise, depending on his count, B may ask for a third card. Then A, having seen the card (if any) drawn by B, may take a third card. The player whose eventual total is nearest to 9 is the winner. If there is a tie, no money passes.

2. Standard Procedure

The layout of a baccarat table is shown on the opposite page.

The numbered spaces at each end, from 1 to 12, signify seat numbers, the object being to identify each

The Burn Cards

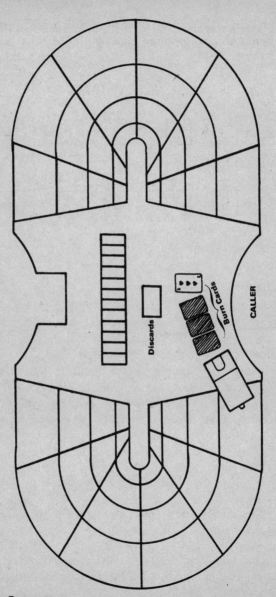

Discards

Burn Cards

CALLER

player's wagers. The words "Bank Hand" in the center indicate where the cards drawn by the bank are displayed. The 12 small boxes in the center are used to indicate the amount of commission due from each player, this commission arising from winning bets on the bank.

The game is operated by three employees. The two dealers in the center collect and pay out wagers. The caller, on the opposite side, directs the game.

Placing of wagers

Players may bet on either "bank" or "player." A bet on the bank is placed in a numbered slot marked "BANK," and a bet on "player" is placed in front of the customer in the space marked "PLAYERS."

Minimum and maximum limits are marked. Baccarat games usually attract the biggest gamblers in a casino.

The shuffle, cut and deal

The game is usually played with 7 or 8 decks, shuffled together.

A joker or otherwise easily distinguishable card is inserted near the end of the combined decks, and the decks are placed in the dealing box known as a "shoe," the same as at the Blackjack table. When later the joker appears, the dealer completes the hand in progress, then reshuffles.

The caller removes the first card from the shoe and turns it face up. The pip value of this card indicates the number of cards to be "burnt"—that is, discarded —before the actual deal begins. In the diagram on the opposite page a 3 is turned up, so three cards are burned before the first hand is dealt.

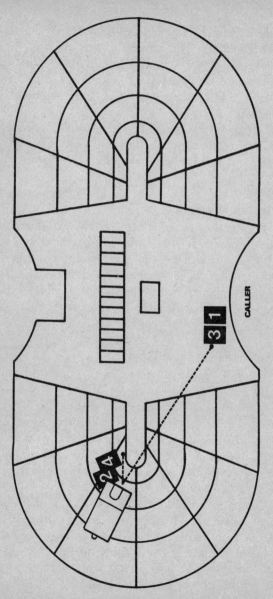

The caller passes the shoe to a player. This player may decline to deal if he wishes, passing the shoe to the player on his right, but players normally deal in their turn. The player dealing handles the cards of the BANK HAND. The dealer must invest at least the table minimum, on whichever side he chooses. So long as the bank hand wins, he may retain the shoe.

When wagers have been placed, the caller says "cards" and the player begins to deal. In the illustration on the opposite page the cards are dealt by the player occupying seat 9.

The dealer directs the first and third cards towards the caller and tucks his own cards beside the shoe. The caller will pass the cards in front of him to another player, usually the customer who has made the largest wager on "Player."

How the play progresses

The customer who holds the "player" cards faces them and tosses them back to the caller, who will lay them down and announce their total. The player with the shoe will then face the two "bank hand" cards and give them to the caller, who will announce the total and display the two hands as shown on page 82.

When either hand holds 8 or 9 in two cards, described as a "Natural," no third card is drawn by either player. In the example above, the Player holds a Natural and is at once declared the winner. When both players hold a Natural, either there will be a tie or Natural 9 will beat Natural 8.

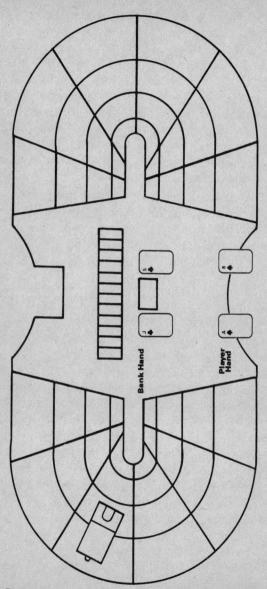

Facing the Hands

3. Drawing a Third Card

When neither side holds a Natural, one or both hands may draw a third card. The decision follows strict rules. On some occasions the decision to stand or draw is palpably illogical, in view of the cards displayed, but the rules follow correct principles of play in Chemin-de-fer, a related game where the original cards are not shown face up and players must act according to probabilities.

Since the caller will direct the play, it is not essential for players to understand the rules that apply. The rules, in fact, are as follows:

The player hand makes the first decision (mandatory, as we have seen). With 0 to 5 he must draw, with 6 or 7 he must stand.

PLAYER HAND THIRD CARD RULES

0 to 5 — Player Hand must draw

6 and 7 — Player Hand must stand

8 and 9 — Natural — both stand

Action by the Bank Hand depends on what the player has done.

(a) When the Player stands

The Bank Hand now follows the same rules, drawing on 0 to 5, standing on 6 or 7.

(b) When the Player draws

The Bank must now draw on 0 to 2, stand on 7. With 3 to 6 his action depends on the card drawn by the player.

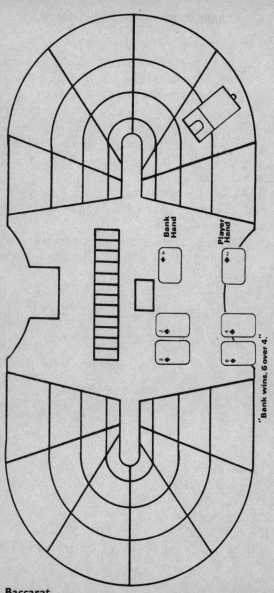

Bank Hand

Player Hand

"Bank wins, 6 over 4."

BANK HAND THIRD CARD RULES

WHEN PLAYER HAND DRAWS
0 to 2 — Bank Hand must draw
3 to 6 — Third card to Player Hand
determines if draw or stand
7 — Bank Hand must stand
8 and 9 — Natural — both hands stand

The next diagram shows the precise action taken by the Bank when the Player has drawn and the Bank holds 3 to 6.

THIRD CARD RULES
WHEN BANK HAND TOTALS 3 to 6

Bank Hand Total	Bank Hand DRAWS if Player Hand Drew	Bank Hand STANDS if Player Hand Drew	
3	1-2-3-4-5-6-7 9-10		8
4	2-3-4-5-6-7	1	8-9-10
5	4-5-6-7	1-2-3	8-9-10
6	6-7	1-2-3-4-5	8-9-10

The numbers on the right half of the diagram naturally complement those on the left. For example, when the player has drawn and the Bank total is 5, the Bank draws on 4 5 6 7 and stands on the other totals.

The diagram opposite shows a situation where both sides, following the rules, have drawn to 2.

Here the caller will announce: "Bank hand wins, 6 over 4."

4. Settlement of Wagers

Despite the rigmarole whereby one player deals from the shoe and another turns up the Player cards, players in this form of baccarat are always betting against the casino, not (as in Chemin-de-fer) against one another. It is in the nature of the game that the Bank has a small advantage. The rules for Bank Hand and Player Hand are different. In the long run, the Bank Hand draws higher average totals, so it wins more than one-half of the hands played.

Gamblers who wager on the Player are thus backing the less favored runner. Players who back the Bank pay 5% commission on winning bets. This amount is not immediately deducted. A player who has invested $20 on a winning Bank bet is paid the full $20, but the dealer will place a commission marker of $1 in the "commission marker box" corresponding to the player's seat number. Between shoes, or when he leaves the table, the player must pay all of his commissions owed to the dealer.

The casino advantage

Although 5% is deducted from winning Bank bets, it must be borne in mind that the Bank has a built-in advantage of about $2\frac{1}{2}$%. The house advantage in baccarat is between 1 and $1\frac{1}{2}$%. A wager on the Bank, despite the commission, is fractionally better than a wager on the Player, but only to the extent of about 1 in 500.

Proposition Bets

Some baccarat layouts offer Proposition Bets, but none of these are standard. One can say about them the same as about the Proposition Bets in Craps: Avoid them!

Roulette

ROULETTE

1. Nature of the Game

Roulette is the oldest and simplest of all the casino games. A roulette table has a wheel with 38 numbered pockets in which a rotating ball may land. The same 38 numbers are displayed on a flat surface, as shown on page 92.

Players place their chips on a selected number or numbers. They win when the ball settles in a pocket which corresponds to the numbers they have backed.

The two zeros

In fact, as the diagram shows, there are 36 numerals, from 1 to 36, plus two zeros, shown on the top, 0 and 00 (double zero). Unless one of these zeros has been specifically backed, the casino sweeps the boards when 0 or 00 turns up. This constitutes the casino's advantage.

If a player places a bet on any of the 36 numbers, he gets paid 35 to 1 when he wins. If he bets on any of the outside panels (Odd–Even, Red–Black, 1–18, etc.) he gets paid even money when he wins. If he bets on 0 or 00, he gets paid 35 to 1 when he wins, but something else happens when the ball lands in the 0 or 00 slot: the even-money players only lose half their bets.

And one more point: In Atlantic City, the casino allows the bettor on even money spots an option: either he can surrender half his bet or leave his bet until the next roll under the so-called "en prison" rule (see page 124 for full explanation).

2. Standard Procedure

Purchasing chips

Roulette chips are usually purchased in stacks of 20. They may be purchased with currency or with chips from other games. Roulette chips have no monetary value printed on them, but they come in different colors and designs and the croupier who operates the table will give the customer a set of chips of declared value. The advantage of this system is that when several chips are placed on the same number by different players, it is clear to whom each chip belongs. A player who is using green chips will of course be paid off with chips of the same color. A marker on the rim of the table may indicate the value attached to the designs.

Placing a bet

When the dealer has paid off all the winners from the previous spin, wagering begins on the next spin. The plastic or metal ball, which is rotated in an opposite direction to the wheel, will take a minute to settle and most betting takes place while the ball is in motion. When the dealer sees that the ball is slowing down he will call "No more bets."

Chip minimum and table minimum

Minimum and maximum limits will be displayed. However, there is a distinction between a table minimum

Inside and Outside Bets

1to18	1st 12	0	00	
		1	2	3
		4	5	6
EVEN		7	8	9
		10	11	12
RED	2nd 12	13	14	15
		16	17	18
BLACK		19	20	21
		22	23	24
ODD	3rd 12	25	26	27
		28	29	30
19to36		31	32	33
		34	35	36
		2to1	2to1	2to1

INSIDE

OUTSIDE

and a chip minimum. A player must always invest an amount equal to the table minimum but may in certain circumstances divide his bet. The diagram opposite shows the difference between "inside" and "outside" bets.

Suppose the table minimum is $2 and the chip minimum $1. A player backing any of the simpler chances, which are found on the "outside," may bet only in units of $2. A player betting on the longer chances "inside" must invest the table minimum but may divide his bet between different numbers.

Payment of winning bets

When the ball has come to rest in its numbered slot, the dealer will announce the number and color (red or black) and point to the number on the table. All winnings on outside bets will be laid alongside the stake and will be left there for the next spin unless they exceed the maximum or the player removes them. Winnings on inside bets (which may be 35 times the original stake) will be passed to the player, but the stake will be left on the table. The player may, of course, remove it before the next spin.

3. Variety of Bets Offered

A single chip, placed in a conventional position, may signify a bet on a group of numbers. It is necessary to understand the system, as otherwise the bet may not reflect the player's intentions.

		0	00	
1to18	1st 12	1	2	3
		4	5	6
EVEN		7	8	9
		10	11	12
RED	2nd 12	13	14	◉
		16	17	18
BLACK		19	20	21
		22	23	24
ODD	3rd 12	25	26	27
		28	29	30
19to36		31	32	33
		34	35	36
		2to1	2to1	2to1

With one minor exception (easily avoided), all bets give the casino the same mathematical advantage. While there are 38 numbers on the wheel and on the table, the casino pays out as though there were only 36. For example, suppose you place a bet on Black. There are 18 Black numbers, 18 Red and 2 (green) zeros. If you win, you are paid out at even money, not at the true odds. (Also, see page 91 regarding 0 and 00.)

Backing a single number

You back a single number (or 0 or 00) by placing a chip in the center of the square representing the number. On the opposite page you have backed 15.

If 15 turns up you will be paid at the rate of 35 to 1. The dealer will pass you 35 chips and leave your stake on the table.

Backing two numbers

You can back two adjacent numbers with a single chip by placing it on the line dividing them. In the example on page 98 you are backing 20 and 23.

As always, the payoff is calculated on the basis of 36 numbers, so this bet pays 34 to 2, or 17 to 1.

The combination 0 and 00 can be backed in the normal way by placing a chip on the line between them, and also, for the convenience of patrons at that end of the table, on the line dividing 2nd 12 and 3rd 12.

Backing three numbers

You can back three numbers with one chip by placing it on the transversal—16 to 18 in the diagram on page 99

Backing Two Numbers

		0	00	
1to18	1st 12	1	2	3
		4	5	6
EVEN		7	8	9
		10	11	12
RED	2nd 12	13	14	15
		16	17	18
BLACK		19	20	21
		22	23	24
ODD	3rd 12	25	26	27
		28	29	30
19to36		31	32	33
		34	35	36
		2to1	2to1	2to1

		0		00
1to18	1st 12	1	2	3
		4	5	6
EVEN		7	8	9
		10	11	12
RED	2nd 12	13	14	15
		16	17	18
BLACK		19	20	21
		22	23	24
ODD	3rd 12	25	26	27
		28	29	30
19to36		31	32	33
		34	35	36
		2to1	2to1	2to1

—and also by placing a chip at one of the junctions between 0 00 1 2 and 3.

The bet pays 33 to 3, or 11 to 1.

Backing four numbers

You can back four adjoining numbers with one chip by placing it at the center of the square that contains them all. In the diagram on the opposite page you are backing the four numbers, 26 27 29 30.

This bet pays 32 to 4, 8 to 1.

Backing five numbers

There is only one way to back five numbers with a single chip. In the diagram on page 102 you are covering 0 00 1 2 and 3.

Since 31 is not exactly divisible by 5, this bet pays 6 to 1, which is slightly under the normal odds. The bet is not to be recommended, because if you placed five separate chips on the five numbers, and one of them turned up, you would win 31 chips instead of 30.

Backing six numbers

A chip covering two transversals is a bet on six numbers, 28 to 33 in the example on page 103.

This bet pays 30 to 6, 5 to 1.

		0		00
1 to 18	**1st 12**	1	2	3
		4	5	6
EVEN		7	8	9
		10	11	12
RED	**2nd 12**	13	14	15
		16	17	18
BLACK		19	20	21
		22	23	24
ODD	**3rd 12**	25	26	27
		28	29	30
19 to 36		31	32	33
		34	35	36
		2 to 1	2 to 1	2 to 1

		0	00	
1 to 18	1st 12	1	2	3
		4	5	6
EVEN		7	8	9
		10	11	12
RED	2nd 12	13	14	15
		16	17	18
BLACK		19	20	21
		22	23	24
ODD	3rd 12	25	26	27
		28	29	30
19 to 36		31	32	33
		34	35	36
		2 to 1	2 to 1	2 to 1

		0	00	
1 to 18	1st 12	1	2	3
		4	5	6
EVEN		7	8	9
		10	11	12
RED	2nd 12	13	14	15
		16	17	18
BLACK		19	20	21
		22	23	24
ODD	3rd 12	25	26	27
		28	29	30
19 to 36		31	32	33
		34	35	36
		2 to 1	2 to 1	2 to 1

103

Backing twelve numbers

We turn now to bets on the "outside," which cover larger groups of numbers. Remember that any bet placed on the outside must be not less than the table minimum.

You may, of course, place a chip on 1st 12, 2nd 12 or 3rd 12, and besides this you may back the twelve numbers in a column, as from 2 to 35, as shown in the diagram on the opposite page.

Thus there are six ways of backing a group of twelve, as shown in the diagram on page 106.

Naturally they all pay the same odds, 2 to 1.

Backing eighteen numbers

Finally, there are the even money chances, where you back eighteen numbers and are paid 1 to 1. You may back 1 to 18, 19 to 36, odd or even, red or black, as shown in the diagram on page 107.

If 0 or 00 turns up, all these bets lose.

You may, of course, back two or three of these even chances; for example, you could place bets on even, black and 19 to 36.

		0	00	
1to18	1st 12	1	2	3
		4	5	6
EVEN		7	8	9
		10	11	12
RED	2nd 12	13	14	15
		16	17	18
		19	20	21
BLACK		22	23	24
ODD	3rd 12	25	26	27
		28	29	30
		31	32	33
19to36		34	35	36
		2to1	2to1	2to1

Six Ways of Backing Twelve Numbers

		0	00	
1 to 18	1st 12 ◎	1	2	3
		4	5	6
EVEN		7	8	9
		10	11	12
RED	2nd 12 ◎	13	14	15
		16	17	18
BLACK		19	20	21
		22	23	24
ODD	3rd 12 ◎	25	26	27
		28	29	30
19 to 36		31	32	33
		34	35	36
		2 to 1	2 to 1	2 to 1

Six Ways of Backing Eighteen Numbers

		0	00	
1 to 18	**1st 12**	1	2	3
		4	5	6
		7	8	9
EVEN		10	11	12
RED	**2nd 12**	13	14	15
		16	17	18
		19	20	21
BLACK		22	23	24
ODD	**3rd 12**	25	26	27
		28	29	30
		31	32	33
19 to 36		34	35	36
		2to1	2to1	2to1

Slot Machines

SLOT MACHINES

Slot players like the exercise of pulling the lever, seeing the pictures roll, and losing their nickels, dimes, quarters, half dollars and/or silver dollars slowly.

Years ago, slot machines were very unimportant revenue producers in Nevada. They had very high percentages, often taking over 20% of the money put in them. In recent years slot machines have been offering much more liberal payoffs and have become more attractive to the customers.

In 1976 the casinos started offering high percentage return dollar slot machines that have swept the Nevada gaming industry. Some casinos return as much as 97% on the dollar, which is almost as good as some of the better table bets. High return 25¢ machines are being introduced that return over 90% on the dollar. With competition these machines might become even more liberal.

The machines are very simple in operation, but they offer different types of rewards. Some machines are loaded with cherry symbols and pay off small amounts frequently. They have few large payoffs, but they give a lot of action to the player because they are paying off regularly. In contrast, there are jackpot-only machines which do not pay off frequently, but offer only large payoffs, and at the extreme, there are the huge progressive jackpots that keep increasing in value every time the handle is pulled. These have resulted in jackpots as high as $250,000 for one handle pull.

If you should hit a jackpot, be sure to call the casino attendant by ringing the button on the machine and wait for him or her before taking your coins from the tray. The reason is that you may be entitled to 250 coins, for example, and the machine may only contain 150. If you take your money and walk away, you may be short-changing yourself. The attendant will pay you in currency the total revealed on your slot machine for the Bar-Bar-Bar or whatever jackpot you hit minus the amount the machine pays in coins.

Staking Systems and Money Management

STAKING SYSTEMS AND MONEY MANAGEMENT

It is time now for some observations on the mathematical and human aspects of casino gambling. First, let us dispose of some false notions relating mostly to roulette.

Dice have no memory

After a run of five Reds, do you think that Red is more or less likely to turn up again? Put like that, you will doubtless agree that the probabilities are unchanged. Exactly! The dice have no memory. Yet in European casinos, where roulette is played in a different style and at a much more leisurely pace than American roulette, you will see half the players recording every spin of the wheel, waiting for the moment when they deem it judicious to enter the fray. Some gamblers will tell you that they never bet "against the wheel," meaning that they follow trends. An equal number will wait, say, for a run of Reds before beginning to support Black. Neither concept has any sense to it.

Staking systems

Millions of words have been written about staking systems, mostly for roulette but applicable to any form of casino gambling. Let us be clear about this: the casino advantage is permanent and insurmountable. Every system has the same probability (certainty, really) of losing in the long run. The timing is different, that is all.

A player can, of course, adopt a method of staking that will make him favorite to win for a fairly long while. Taking advantage of the very big difference between minimum and maximum limits at a casino, he may follow a method of increasing stakes that will enable him to be a small winner on 100 days in succession; but on the 101st day there will be a hostile run and he will lose more than he has won on all the other days. And the calamitous run might, of course, occur on Day 1.

The snag in all doubling-up systems is easily seen if one observes how quickly the risk mounts. Suppose you go to a casino intending to lose not more than, say, $200. You invest $1 on an even chance (well, nearly even), proposing, if it loses, to invest $2 next time, then $4, and so on. After seven losing coups you will either have to give up or go beyond your limit and invest 255 units. And in 200 coups the odds are better than 3 to 1 that there will be a run of seven against you.

Systems that involve an increase *when winning*— for example, letting the money stand after a winning coup in Roulette or Blackjack—have a better psychological sense. At least, you will be plunging with the casino's money.

However, let it not be thought that any staking system erodes the house advantage. The author has a friend who wrote a learned book describing, with numerous mathematical tables, how to win at roulette. Well, he has the Old Age Pension to console him now.

The "come back tomorrow" theory

Next, there are those who speak and write with all seriousness about "patterns" and "rhythm" and "form" and "self-discipline." They observe "rhythm" in the roulette wheels, they increase their stakes when "in form," they stop playing when "out of form," they do not exceed their daily limit. In the days before gaming was allowed in Britain one often used to hear of shrewd folk who spent the winter in the south of France, "winning their little bit every day at the casino." Three observations may be made about that:

(1) Most gamblers are liars.

(2) It is in the interest of the casinos to encourage, or at least not to deny, such tales.

(3) It is consistent with the laws of probability that one or two people in every thousand should be a good deal luckier than the average.

The absurdity of the "come back tomorrow when my luck will be better" theory is easily seen if one reflects on it in this way: Suppose *all* the players at the table exhibited this type of human wisdom and restraint. Would they all be winners? The chips on the table don't share the psychological problems of the people who placed them there—they are just chips!

Money management

Money management is a different affair. This is exhibited not by any particular method of staking but by hazarding no more than one is prepared to lose with equanimity. Certainly it is sensible, when you go to a casino for an evening or longer, to decide how much you intend to risk, and stick to it. It is all too easy, when handling chips, to lose all sense of what they represent in daily toil. There is much to be said, also, for "garaging" (a term used in Chemin-de-fer). This means, if you find you are winning, garage your original capital and in no circumstances break into it.

In the end, there's only one good chance to come out a winner, and that is to bet seldom. If you sit at the table for hours and make hundreds of bets in the course of the session you have a very small chance to beat the percentage. If you intend to risk, say, $100 altogether on the day's play, ideally your best plan is to put it all on one of the bets that have only a small casino advantage. However, you are there for amusement, so you will probably want to make at least a few wagers. It is better, by far, to make ten bets of $10 each than a hundred of $1 each.

European Scene

THE EUROPEAN SCENE

American visitors will find most of their favorite games in Britain and France. Blackjack, Roulette, and Baccarat, in one of its forms, are played everywhere. Craps is comparatively rare, but there are Crap tables in some London casinos and in Monte Carlo. Keno is not played at all.

The French and British casinos are controlled by strict regulations and some offer better odds to the gambler than American casinos. Casinos in Belgium, Italy and Germany operate in the French style, but in countries where gaming is found only in a few tourist resorts the odds tend to be poor.

When you go to a French casino for the first time you will need your passport. If you don't go again for twenty years you will find they still know about you! In Britain, also, you cannot walk in off the street. There is a strict 48-hour rule, whose effect is that you must give notice in advance of your intention to take part in gaming. Travel agents and hotels can organize this on your behalf. You can, however, play immediately if introduced by a club member. The staff who operate the gaming tables are forbidden to accept tips, and, far different from Nevada casinos, no alcoholic refreshments are served on any floor that is licensed for gaming.

There are slight differences in the style of play between American and European casinos. We comment on these differences below, concerning ourselves not with small details of procedure but with such differences as affect the odds. We also describe the game of *Trente-et-quarante*.

Blackjack

In European Blackjack it is usual to play with four decks and the croupier will cut off a substantial number of cards to make any system of counting less effective.

All cards are dealt face upwards and the dealer does not take his own second card until all the players have completed their hands. The dealer does not (as in America) declare his own Blackjack in advance. It therefore becomes unwise to double down with 11 against an Ace and borderline to double down against a 10.

In Britain, the Gaming Board makes certain regulations that are designed to inform and aid inexperienced players. Doubling down is allowed only with totals of 11 10 and 9. This saves players from committing certain follies but it also prevents them from doubling down with soft hands between A 2 and A 7.

The Gaming Board prohibits the splitting of 4-4 5-5 and 10-10. This is sound advice for the most part, though there is said to be a minimal advantage in splitting 4-4 against dealer's 5.

Insurance bets are not allowed, on the grounds that it is normally disadvantageous to take odds of 2 to 1 about a 9 to 4 chance. Professional players complain of this since it prevents them from benefiting from special situations where the deck is 10-rich and the odds below 2 to 1, but their pleas have so far been disregarded.

Craps

British Crap games usually take 1-1 instead of 6-6 as the barred bet in Don't Pass and Don't Come, but there is no technical difference in this. The casino advantage in Field Bets is generally reduced by including 5 rather than 4 in the Field. Alternatively, when 4 is part of the Field and 5 is not, the casino will pay double on 1-1 and double or even triple on 6-6. Proposition bets are allowed, but the odds are more realistic than in American casinos.

Punto Banco, Baccarat and Chemin-de-Fer

Punto Banco, which is the same as American Baccarat, is now the commonest form of Baccarat in Britain.

In **Baccarat à tables deux,** a professional dealer, sitting between two tables with spaces for six players at each, plays the Bank Hand, on Punto Banco principles, against two sets of opponents. Whereas in Punto Banco the play follows prescribed rules, in Baccarat both the player and the dealer have certain options.

An interesting situation may arise where the correct play for the dealer against Table 1 may be to take a third card, against Table 2 to stand. In such a case he will make the correct play against the Table on which most money has been wagered. Consequently, there is a minimal advantage in supporting the Table that carries less money, because the dealer will occasionally make an inferior play against that Table.

Chemin-de-fer is the same game in essence, but now the shoe passes among the players. The player who has the shoe plays the Bank Hand against one of the other players, usually his right-hand neighbor. The players have options in a few situations where there is very little to choose between one play and another. When the banker wins the coup he may continue to run his bank. After a few coups he is allowed to "garage" a part of his winnings, or he may pass the bank. When the player opposing the bank does not wish to play for the full amount, anyone at the table (or outside it) may call "Banco" and play alone against the bank.

The casino does not take part in the play but deducts 5% from winning coups by the Banker. The game has more cumulative excitement than *Punto Banco* or Baccarat, because the Bank may run high. The word *Chemin-de-fer* means "railway" and relates to the way in which the shoe circulates around the table. The game is popularly known as "shemmy."

Roulette

In European roulette there is only one zero and the order of numbers on the wheel is different, as will be seen from the illustration on the opposite page.

Impair and *pair* stand for odd and even, and the signs 12p 12m and 12d signify first (*première*), middle and last (*dernière*) dozen.

It will be observed that there is only one zero. This reduces the customer's disadvantage from 5.26% to 2.70%. In addition, losing bets on the even chances (Red, Odd and 1-18) are not immediately surrendered but are placed *"en prison"*—imprisoned. They are placed on the line bordering the bet. If the bet wins on the next spin, the player gets his money back. If zero turns up again, then he will need two winning spins to retrieve his stake. The effect of this *en prison* rule is that the house advantage on even chances is only 1.35%. (Readers of Ian Fleming's book, *Casino Royale*, may recall that the hero's winning method was to back two of the "dozens" at the same time. It would have been more astute to place three-quarters of the stake

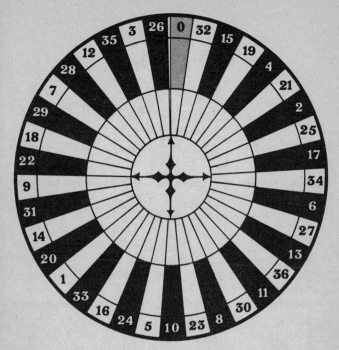

European Roulette Wheel

on 1-18 or 19-36 and the remaining quarter on the *sixaine* required to complete the 24 numbers. This way, he would have stood to benefit from the *en prison* concession on the even chances.)

In French roulette the chips have their value inscribed on them and players do not, as in America, have their own separate stacks. What in Britain is described as American roulette is in fact French roulette played with an American style of staking cloth, which makes for faster work by the croupier.

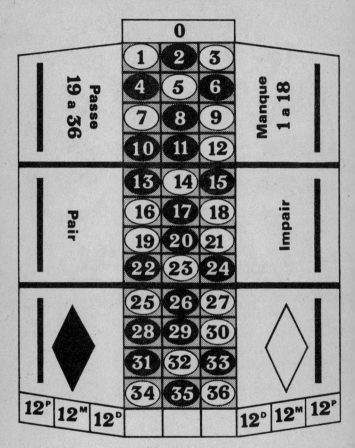

European Roulette Table

Trente-et-quarante

The game of *trente-et-quarante* (30 and 40) is not played in Britain but is played in all French casinos and in Monte Carlo. It is favored by big gamblers because the house advantage is small and because the action is much faster than in French roulette.

The dealer, using undersized cards, deals two rows, stopping at once when the pips in a row total 31 or more. Thus the only possible totals (since picture or court cards count as 10 and Aces as 1) are from 31 to 40. The top row is "black," the second row "red." The row whose total is nearest to 31 wins the coup.

The player may back "black" or "red" to win. He may also leave the decision in the hand of the fates by backing *couleur*, which means that he will be on the row signified by the color of the first card dealt, or *inverse*, meaning that he will be on the opposite color to that of the first card. For example, if the first card dealt is red, and the player has backed *inverse*, his money will be on black, the top row.

The house advantage occurs when both rows total 31. In this case bets are imprisoned, so the player in effect loses half his stake. It should be noted that a tie at 31 is appreciably more likely than a tie at a higher number, such as 38 or 39, which can be reached only in particular circumstances. A player can insure against his bet being imprisoned by adding an amount equivalent to one-hundredth of his stake. It will be seen from this that the casino does not make a big profit on turnover. On the other hand, the game proceeds at a very fast rate, so the player plays many more coups than in other games.

Bonne chance!

Index